THE NEW YORKER
BOOK OF BUSINESS CARTOONS

BLOOMBERG PRESS

PRINCETON

THE
NEW YORKER
BOOK OF BUSINESS CARTOONS

EDITED BY ROBERT MANKOFF

INTRODUCTION BY DAVID REMNICK

PUBLISHED BY BLOOMBERG PRESS

First edition published 1998

1 3 5 7 9 10 8 6 4 2

The New Yorker book of business cartoons / introduction
    by David Remnick ; [edited by Robert Mankoff]. -- 1st
    ed.
        p.   cm.
    Includes index.
    ISBN 1-57660-056-4 (alk. paper)
    1. Business--Caricatures and cartoons. 2. American
wit and humor, Pictorial.   I. Mankoff, Robert.
II. New Yorker (New York, N.Y. : 1925)
NC1428.N47   1998
741.5'973--dc21   98-33461
                                                              CIP

Book Design by Laurie Lohne / Design It Communications

THE
NEW YORKER
BOOK OF BUSINESS CARTOONS

By David Remnick
Editor of *The New Yorker*

*I*f you've ever had occasion to visit the editorial offices of *The New Yorker* on West 43rd Street there is a good chance you will have been greeted at the door by a courtly gentleman who wears a bow tie and a two- or three-piece suit to work. He goes by the initials C.S., and he has more layers of irony to his personality than a napoleon has layers of pastry and cream. While he must let everyone in the door and out, while he is charged with dealing with the winded bike messengers and the rare irate contributor (the rejection letter now clutched like an accordioned dagger in the visitor's reddening paw), one cannot say the task is too taxing, and the lack of activity has allowed him to be the most voracious reader at the magazine.

The only time I have ever seen C.S. at a loss was on my very first day of work as a staff writer at *The New Yorker*. It was a Tuesday, the day the cartoonists leave their garrets in Brooklyn and Manhattan, their studios in Connecticut and Westchester, and come to the office to show their week's work and hope for a sale. This is an old tradition at the magazine. Nowadays, the artists could surely send their work in electronically, but there is, for most of them, an urgent need to escape the close air of the studio, go to the city, and meet with their own species for lunch, not least to trade gossip and size up the competition. There is also a sense among some of the artists that showing up can't hurt, commercially speaking; it might be the extra impetus for the editors to buy their latest cartoon and run it in the magazine sometime soon—perhaps before the Yom Kippur holiday.

The morning I first encountered this ritual, a group of 15 or 20 artists were happily yammering away on the couches behind C.S.'s desk and drinking the brown-paint coffee the magazine provides. Unlike the writers who come to the office daily, the better to escape domestic chaos for the quiet, the cartoonists talk with a sense of gay occasion.

By way of introduction, C.S. closed his book (this time it was Matthew Arnold's *Culture and Anarchy*) and gestured, ironically, over his shoulder.

"One adores them," he said, "but one yearns for solitude."

I knew right away who they were. The cartoonists will hate to hear this (not that this will be the first time) but it really is uncanny the way so many of them look as though they've stepped out of their own drawings. Without being introduced to any of the artists, I could easily recognize some: there was the tall and aristocratic Bill Hamilton, a silk handkerchief peeking out of the breast pocket of his linen blazer; there was shaggy Ed Koren, just down from Vermont, the nettles barely combed from his mustache; and there was flaxen-haired Roz Chast, the magazine's one certifiable genius, and the one cartoonist who will never look quite old enough to qualify for a driver's license.

Later, after the cartoonists had gone off to their meetings with the art editor—it was Lee Lorenz then; it's Bob Mankoff now—I confessed to a friend at the magazine that so long as John Updike kept his distance (there is something deflating about meeting a writer who is Michael Jordan to your Luc Longley), the only *New Yorker* contributors I was wary of meeting were the cartoonists. Not just Roz Chast or Bill Hamilton or Bud Handelsman—the whole lot of them.

First, there is the jealousy factor, the sneaking suspicion that while our subscribers may say that they are buying *The New Yorker* for the fiction, the poetry, the criticism, and the reporting pieces, we, the writers and editors, have this unwavering knowledge that what our readers turn to first is the cartoons. The cartoons are the magazine's emblems, and much of its uniqueness. Even in the age of Comedy Central and 24-hour stand-up channels and all the supersaturation of the airwaves with laugh tracks, the cartoons persist. I've seen *New Yorker* cartoons taped up on countless refrigerators and bathroom walls; on the doors of insurance adjusters and professors of comparative barbering. It will never quite be that way for the writers. I'm still looking for that refrigerator decorated with a "Letter from Moscow."

Second, there is an envy of a more profound kind. The best cartoons have about them a sense of effortlessness, as if they were pieces of found art. They seem so stark and simple, like a small bomb. The combination of ink drawing and a few words produce a kind of explosive release—laughter—and truth all at once. Something so simple must be near impossible to do. My colleagues and I routinely give lip service to the art of concision—good taste dictates Flaubert over Hugo—but what writer isn't always *hokking* an editor for more space? As a writer, I have been guilty of it. We are road hogs, forever trying to occupy the whole highway, and so when we see the magical effects the cartoonists get with their drawings and their combustible bits of language, we begin to wonder about our own failings, the grossness of our 10,000- and 20,000-word bloviations.

A final reason for envy—and this is the raison d'être for the book you hold in your hands—is that the cartoonists at *The New Yorker* have "covered" an entire world, the business world, far better, far more profoundly and more consistently, than have the writers over the magazine's long history. In no small measure, our readers live in a daytime world that has escaped our understanding, a world more obscure to us than quantum mechanics. It is hard to know how many of our readers work in offices, those great emotional and professional petri dishes laid end to end from Manhattan to Honolulu, but it is surely a high proportion. Over the years, the magazine's writers have traveled to Patagonia; Holcomb, Kansas; and Mont Blanc for their stories, but only rarely to where our readers spend their days. As a rule, we are better at illuminating the world of the Eskimo fisherman or St. Petersburg painter than that of the Philadelphia accountant or the Wichita CEO.

There have been some exceptions. Wolcott Gibbs is probably best known for his lampoon of Henry Luce and the peculiar folkways of Time-Life. John Brooks wrote about the atmosphere of triumph in "The Go-Go Years" in the Sixties (that's when Wall Street was thrilled with a Dow of nearly 1,000). Tom Whiteside, who died not long ago, wrote well about advertising, and John Bainbridge about the business of Texans. But for the most part, Harold Ross and William Shawn did not go looking for business writing. The subject was considered dry, philistine, uninteresting. On the fiction side, plenty of John Cheever's and John O'Hara's men were men of the business world (the women were still at home) but their dramas and horrors nearly all came after work.

I think the aversion to business also had more than a little to do with class and snobbery. Although the staff of *The New Yorker* numbered not a few men and women born to money or at least shabby gentility, a distaste for commerce was, stylistically, de rigueur. The editors and writers were well aware that their readers were of the business class—if not, then why was the magazine so successful in garnering glossy ads from Cadillac, Merrill Lynch, Tiffany, and Bergdorf Goodman? And yet the magazine's pioneering voices in the Harold Ross years, E. B. White and James Thurber, celebrated their own inability to balance a checkbook. An executive, in their eyes, was a kind of unfortunate bumbler, a pitiful blowhard heading back to Grand Central stunned by his hopelessly banal workday and his three-martini lunch. In part, *The New Yorker* was what you read to lift you out of the business world, to leave it behind for a few hours before trudging once more to the station and the 7:10 to Grand Central.

Then came the 1980s, and the subject of money in American life—its dominance, its folly—became unavoidable. There had always been, it seemed, *Forbes* and *Fortune* and *Business Week,* straight-up accountings of the commercial world. Now the field grew more crowded and the writing more vivid and varied. A magazine called *Manhattan,inc.* started profiling business tycoons with the idea that they could surely be as interesting as movie stars, professional athletes, and politicians. Who were these tycoons? Where did their fortunes come from? What were they like? What language did they speak? What were their habits and ambitions? *Vanity Fair,* a revived magazine, went back and forth between celebrating the nouveaux riches and poking fun at them. The satirical magazine *Spy* threw darts at all the puffery of the era, and was especially fast to disdain the gaudy arrivistes in favor of dandruff-flecked Old Money. *Rolling Stone* wisely published the pop novel of the era, Tom Wolfe's *The Bonfire of the Vanities*, in serialized form. Wolfe, unlike O'Hara or Cheever, took the readers into the office and sat them in front of those blinking screens where traders make their piles.

Finally, *The New Yorker* got into the act. Mark Singer wrote a brilliant saga of the rise and collapse of a bank in Oklahoma and called it "Funny Money." Connie Bruck wrote stunning accounts of the culture within Time Warner and of a Wall Street manic-depressive. Ever since, business has been a staple of *New Yorker* writing, with Bruck, Singer, James Stewart, Ken Auletta, and John Cassidy reporting on that world from their various angles of vision. And yet *The New Yorker*'s most original business "writing" has for a long time been in its art. The *New Yorker* cartoon has traditionally employed a variety of tropes and landscapes—the desert island, the bar, the marital (and nonmarital) bed—but the place where the magazine's readers spend the most time, I'm sure, is the field of commerce: the office, the boardroom. *The New Yorker*'s cartoonists, each in his or her own way, have seized on the business world and found laughter in its codes, clichés, rivalries, desperations, vanities, anxieties, and power relations.

Bob Mankoff, who selects the cartoons for the magazine, selected the cartoons for this book, too. He's also drawn some of the funniest cartoons on business ever published in *The New Yorker*. His specialty is his ability to identify a phrase, a voguish morsel of talk, from the business universe and nudge it into the realm of absurdity. In one cartoon, Mankoff has an executive at his desk talking sternly into his telephone: "A billion is a thousand million? Why wasn't I informed of this?" In a stroke the archetypal boss, demanding always to be kept in the loop, is made a fool. In another, an executive is stopped outside his office by his secretary, who earnestly informs him, "Sir, the following paradigm shifts occurred while you were out." In both, Mankoff seizes on the familiar and the bogus ("Why wasn't I informed of this?" and "paradigm shifts") and yanks them in such a way that the humor is in the despair of the executive who is eternally on edge. In another cartoon, a Mankoff classic, an executive at his desk consults his calendar and tells someone on the phone, "No, Thursday's out. How about never—is never good for you?" What's funny here, of course, is the way in which the euphemisms of biz-talk are always one small step from bloody disdain.

Since the Depression, a constant theme of business humor has been the fear of falling into the lower depths of ruin, the fine line between the penthouse and selling apples on the street. In one of Robert Weber's drawings a hostess prompts her respectable-looking husband at their cocktail party, saying, "Sweetie, show the Hazlitts the watercolors you made in jail." Lee Lorenz has a hopeful-looking guy at an employment agency, where a blasé fellow searches through his card file and says, "I may have something rather outside your field. Would you consider indentured servitude?" The strains and absurdities of the business life are often so onerous that they carry over into the home, where one of Leo Cullum's businessmen-at-rest slumps in his armchair and faces the family dog as if it were an employee in jeopardy: "You've been with us a long time, Winnie," he says, "and we're prepared to offer you a generous severance package."

The cartoonists have also made high comedy of the boomer generation's habit of forever having its cake and eating it, too: all those downtown executives who wear an Armani suit and a ponytail as indicators that while they are in the business world they are not of it. Ed Koren, that great bard of downtown fuzzy urbanity, shows one of his characters, a stockbroker (and surely a former longhair) sitting in his kids' room and, still dressed in bow tie and suspenders, telling them a bedtime story: "And after the prime rate declined by half a point, and the Dow rose by thirty-two, guess what happened to Goose and Fox?" Several of the cartoonists have also found comedy in the rise of women in the executive world. I especially love Warren Miller's captionless drawing of the new Cinderella: a young woman being changed into a would-be CEO by her fairy godmother.

So you can see the source of my anxiety. For more than a decade now, the stock market and every other index have been telling us a historic tale of economic boom (for those at the top). At the same time there has been an unsettling shift in business mores—the end of company loyalty, a permanent sense of impermanence. From the very beginning, it's been the artists, the cartoonists, who have been on the case. We writers and editors have only begun to get at those stories. And yet it may not be a game worth pursuing. What 1,000 words, what 10,000 words, can compete with Tom Cheney's drawing on page 54? In a warren of cubicles, a maze of "workstations," there is one station that has no exit, and inside it sits a skeleton. Meanwhile all the others work on, oblivious to their rotted-out neighbor.

We call these "cartoons," a word that shrugs off pretensions of importance. But they are perhaps the most important thing *The New Yorker* publishes. And I say the hell with it.

"It's up to you now, Miller. The only thing that can save us
is an accounting breakthrough."

"I can't help that. These invoices have to be in the mail tonight."

"Here come the suits."

"*Miss Caldwell, write twenty letters, make five Xerox copies of each, feed the whole lot into the shredder, and then, if it's five o'clock, you may go home.*"

"Pendleton, as of noon today your services will no longer be
required. Meanwhile, keep up the good work."

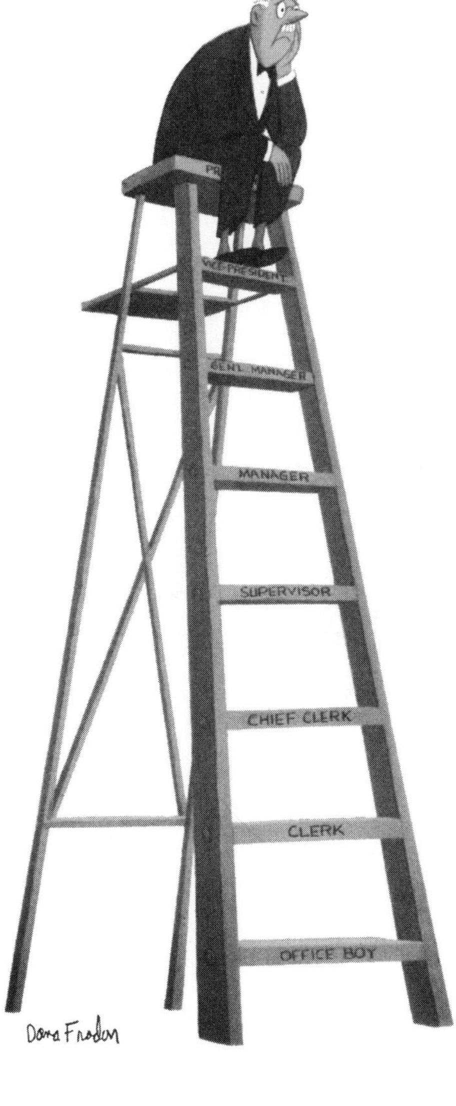
GEN'L MANAGER
MANAGER
SUPERVISOR
CHIEF CLERK
CLERK
OFFICE BOY
Dana Fradon

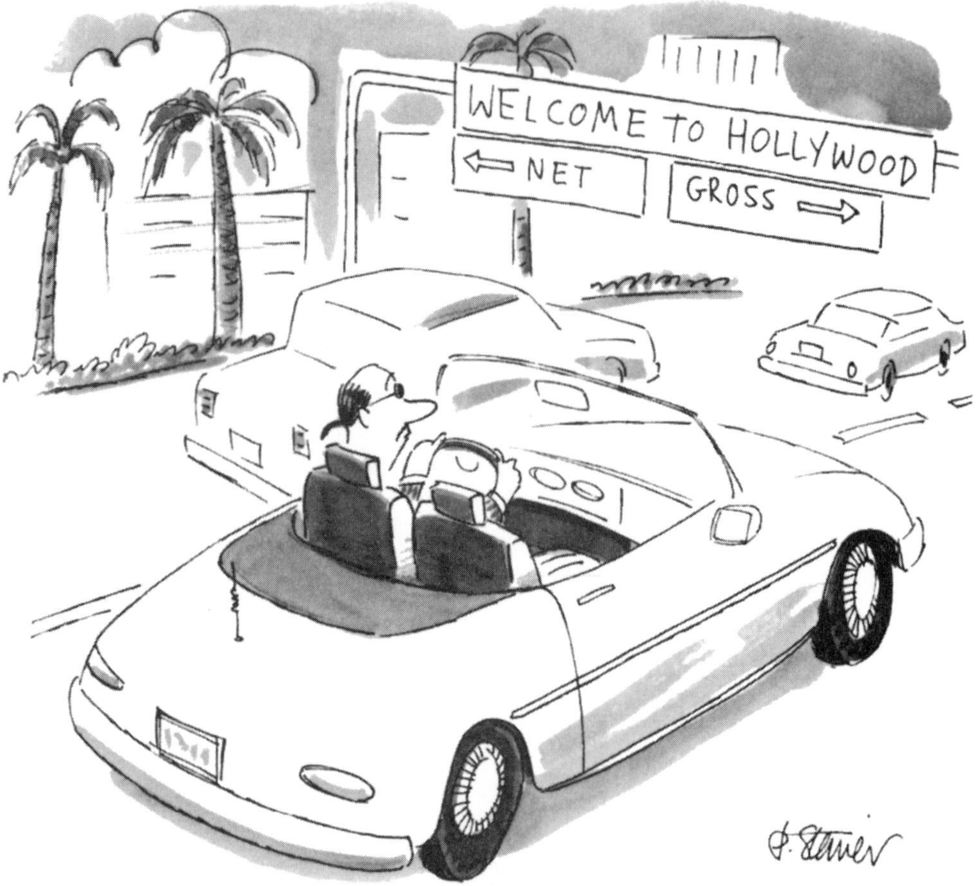
WELCOME TO HOLLYWOOD
NET
GROSS

"Has there been any unusual activity in our stock? The canary just died."

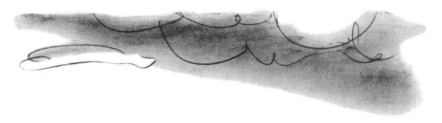

"*Excuse me, sir. I am prepared to make you a rather attractive offer for your square.*"

"Actually, Tommy, we're just about full-blooded management, except for your grandfather on your mom's side, who was one-quarter labor."

"That, my son, is where they store all the minutes
of all the last meetings."

"We are neither hunters nor gatherers. We are accountants."

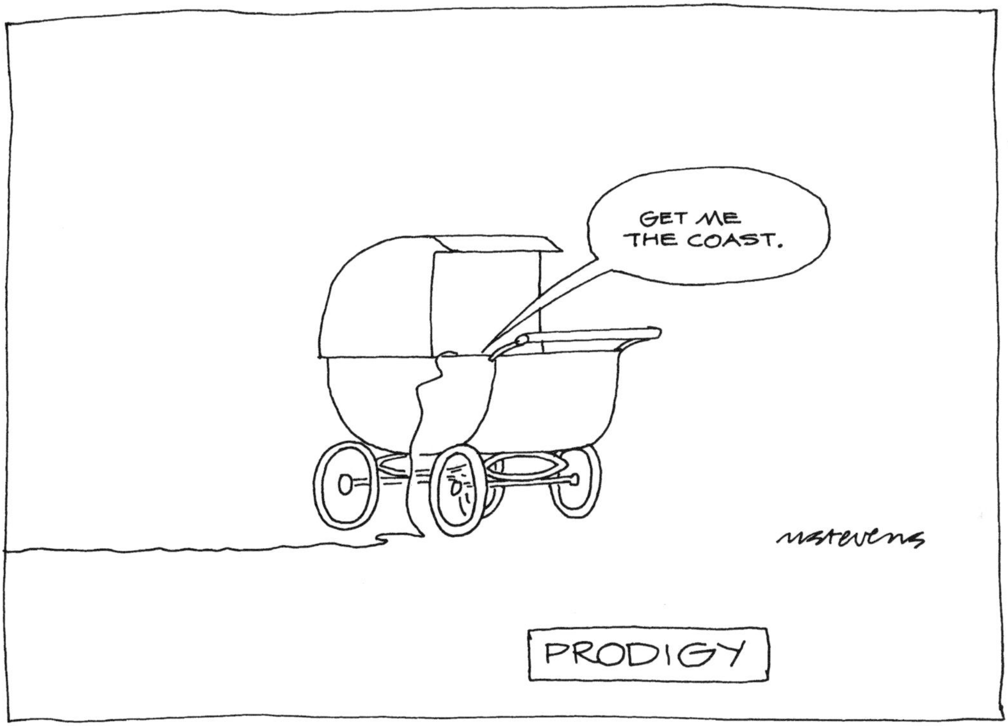
GET ME
THE COAST.
PRODIGY
nstevens

"Basic economics—sometimes the parts are worth more than the whole."

"They say that if she starts playing with her earrings you're dead."

"Sweetie, show the Hazlitts the watercolors you made in jail."

"No, Thursday's out. How about never—is never good for you?"

"Yes, we are going through the same things in life,
but you're going through them at ninety-five thousand dollars a year,
and I'm going through them at thirty-two thousand."

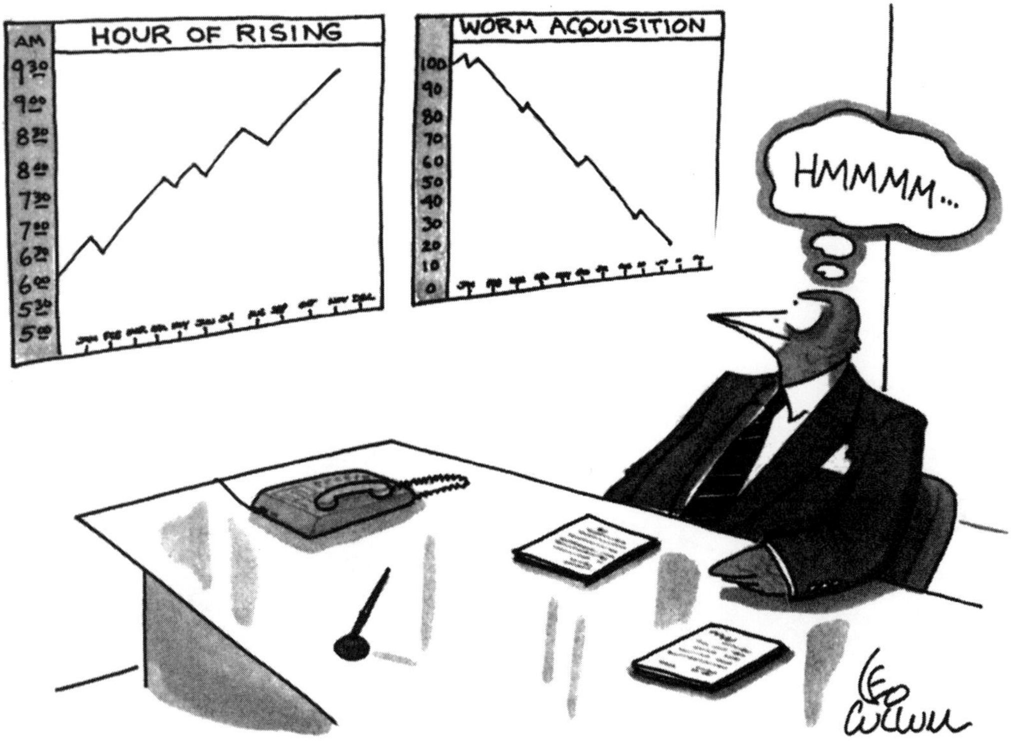
HOUR OF RISING
AM
WORM ACQUISITION
HMMMM...

"I don't know how it started, either. All I know is that it's part of our corporate culture."

"Fenwick, Benton & Perkins. How may I direct your call?"

"It's such a nice day. Why don't you go outside and make some money?"

"*I may have something rather outside your field.*
Would you consider indentured servitude?"

"Gotta run, Peter. A new client is on his way up."

"*I don't get it. Our first three quarters were excellent.*"

"Trust me Mort—no electronic-communications superhighway, no matter how vast and sophisticated, will ever replace the art of the schmooze."

"On the one hand, eliminating the middleman would result in lower costs, increased sales, and greater consumer satisfaction; on the other hand, we're the middleman."

*"I've always had this dream of buying a little farm
and then selling it off piece by piece."*

"Oh, not bad. The light comes on, I press the bar, they write me a check. How about you?"

"No, not there, please. That's where I'm going to put my head."

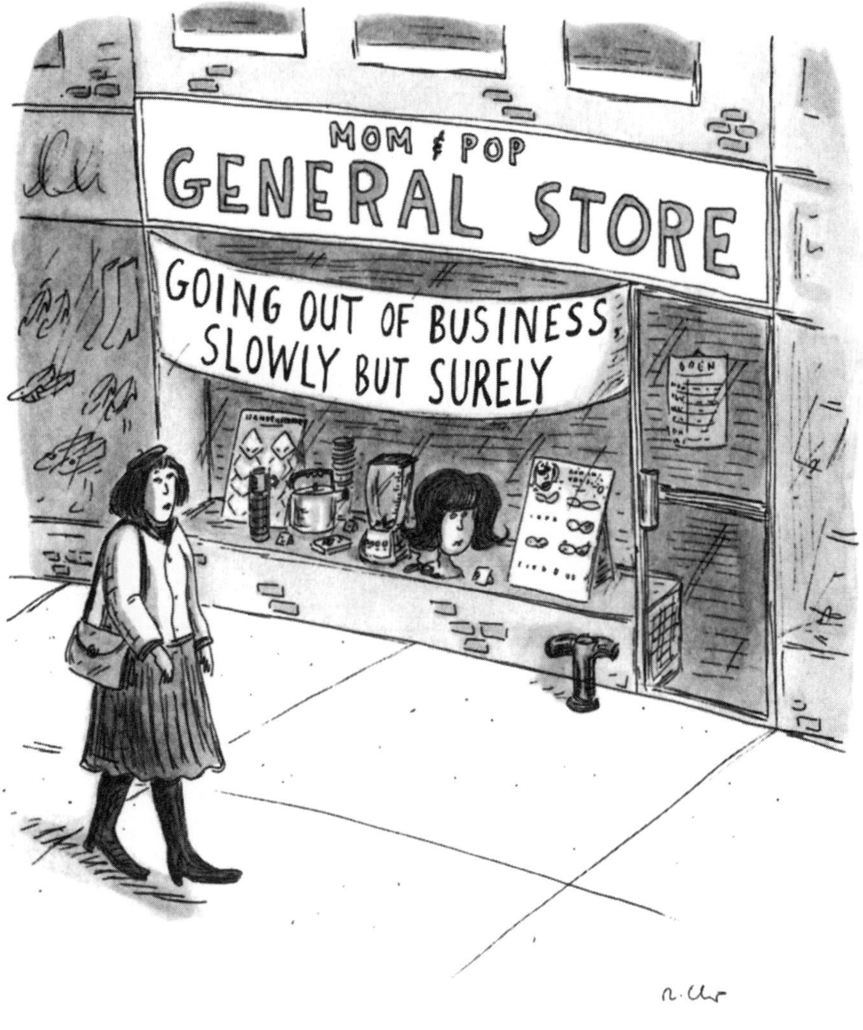
MOM & POP
GENERAL STORE
GOING OUT OF BUSINESS
SLOWLY BUT SURELY

"*If Anderson is C.E.O., and Wyatt is C.F.O., and you're C.O.O., then who am I, and what am I doing here?*"

"Will you stop bothering us? We already have a brokerage firm."

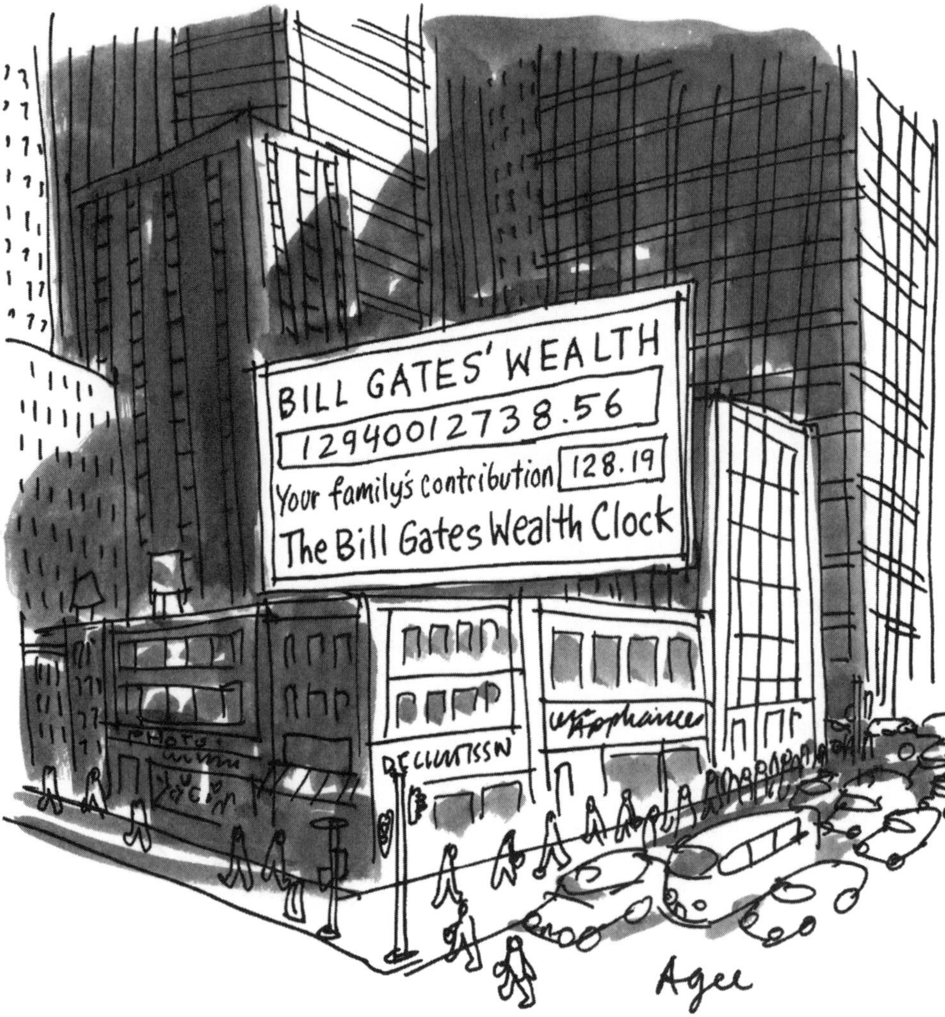
BILL GATES' WEALTH
12940012738.56
Your family's contribution 128.19
The Bill Gates Wealth Clock
Agee

"I think I preferred it <u>before</u> he became an equal-opportunity employer."

"*We younger fleas demand a bigger say in the running of this dog.*"

"And before you know it you're looking at everyone as a commission."

"Millions is craft. Billions is art."

"In six more weeks, these M.B.A.s will be ready for market."

"Wentworth, could I take another look at that reorganization plan?"

"Sir, the following paradigm shifts occurred while you were out."

CORPORATE LEADERS GATHER IN A FIELD OUTSIDE DARIEN, CONNECTICUT, WHERE ONE OF THEM CLAIMS TO HAVE SEEN THE INVISIBLE HAND OF THE MARKETPLACE.

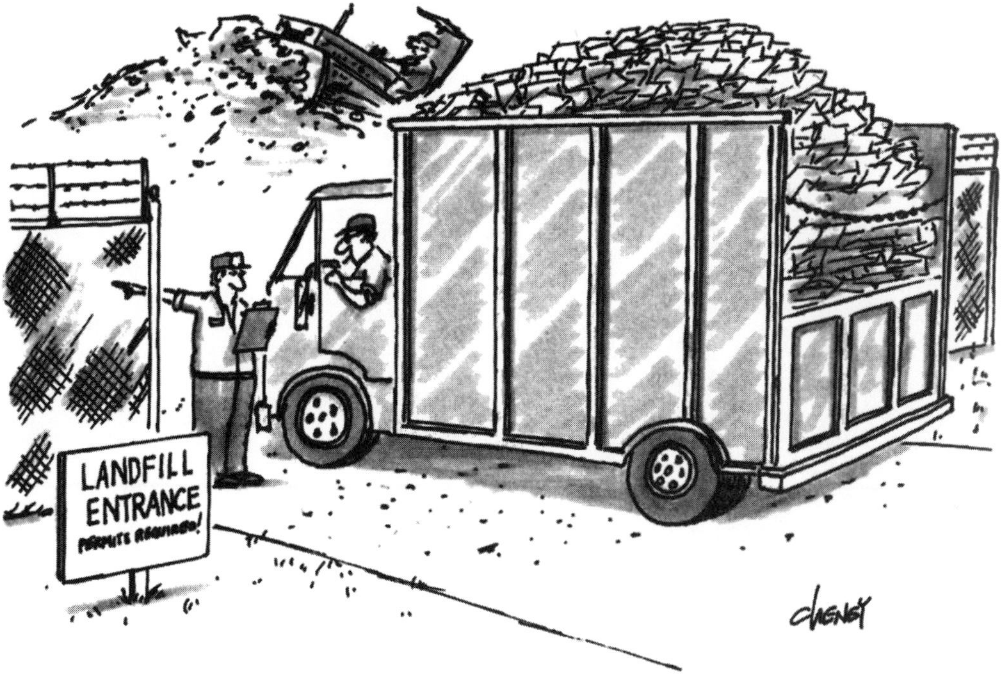
LANDFILL
ENTRANCE
PERMITS REQUIRED!

"Résumés over there."

"This might not be ethical. Is that a problem for anybody?"

"*We have two offices throughout the world.*"

"Try as we might, sir, our team of management consultants has been unable to find a single fault in the manner in which you conduct your business. Everything you do is a hundred per cent right. Keep it up! That will be eleven thousand dollars."

"On the other hand, it's nice to see women in positions
that go beyond mere tokenism."

"A billion is a thousand million? Why wasn't I informed of this?"

"*This is neither Heaven nor Hell. It's the private sector.*"

"You know, the idea of taxation _with_ representation doesn't appeal to me very much, either."

"What a delightful surprise. I always thought it just trickled down to the poor."

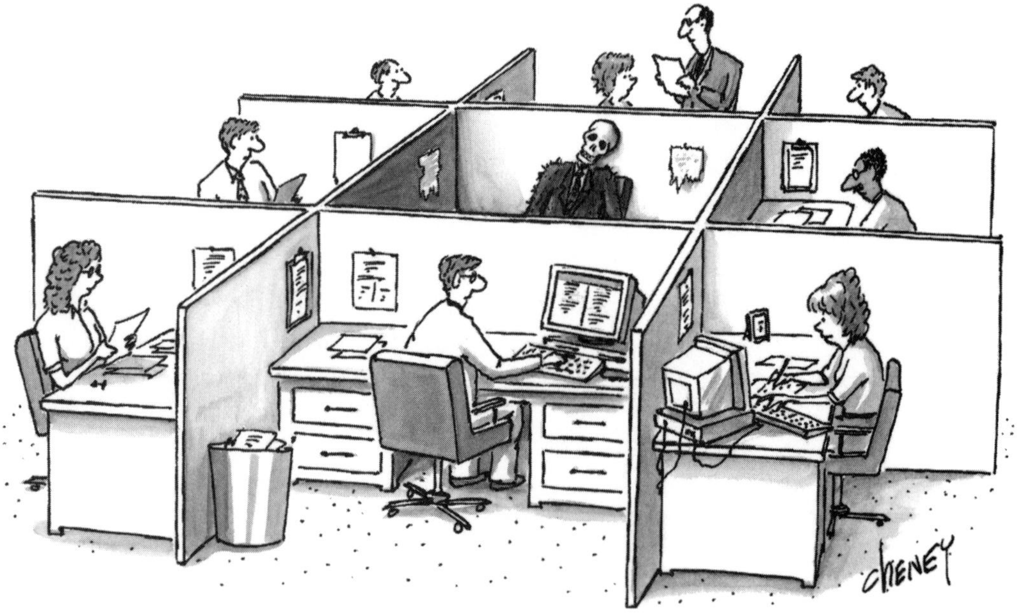
CHENEY

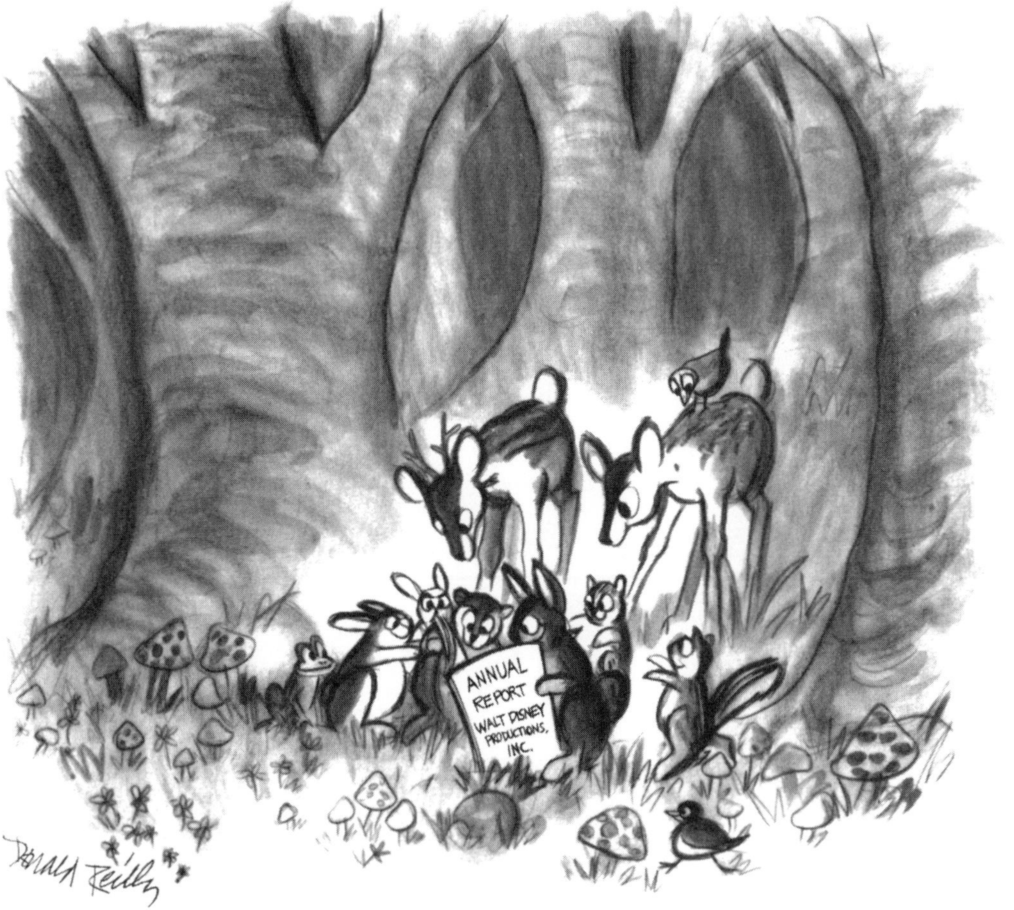
ANNUAL
REPORT
WALT DISNEY
PRODUCTIONS,
INC.

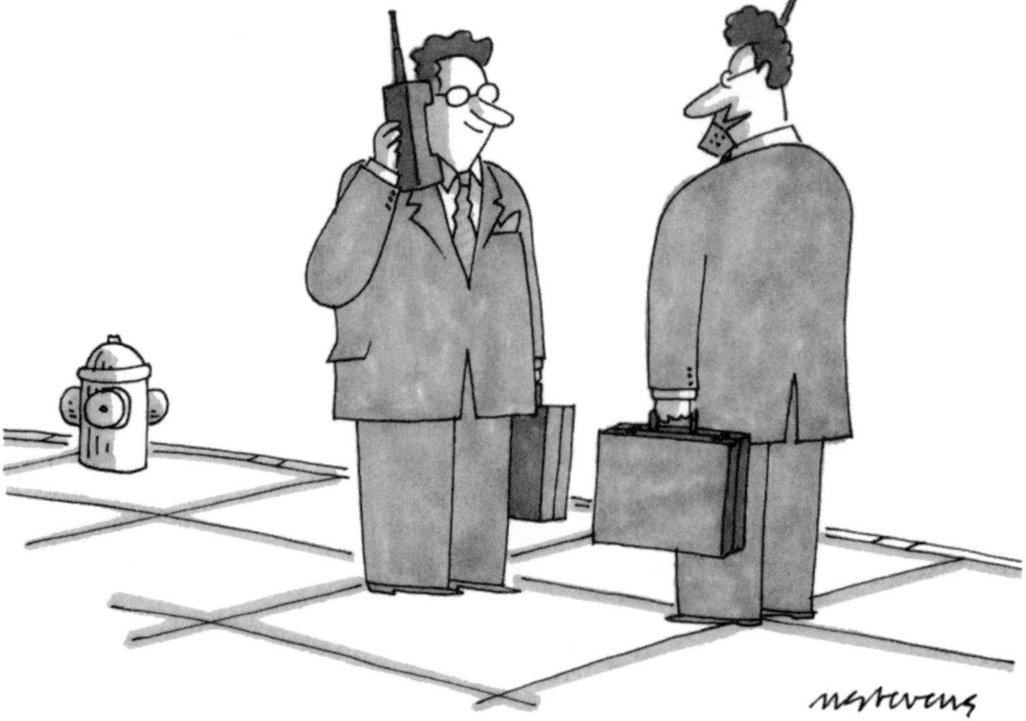
MStevens

"Nice talking to you, Al!"

"*Do you, Scofield Industries, take Amalgamated Pipe?*"

"*Are we thinking here, or is this just so much pointing and clicking?*"

"How is the dollar trading against the Martini today, Jack?"

"Mr. Herman, you made me laugh and you made me cry,
but you didn't make me money."

"Oh, hiring's O.K., but firing provides a real sense of closure."

"I was on the cutting edge. I pushed the envelope. I did the heavy lifting. I was the rainmaker. Then I ran out of metaphors."

"You drive yourself too hard. You really must learn to take
time to stop and smell the profits."

"The tumult and the shouting dies; The captains and the kings depart."

"Something's happened, Doug. I've lost touch with the Warren Buffett in me."

"You see, Thomas, there's a bully at Daddy's office."

"I've never said this to a woman before, but here goes: We're not paying you enough."

"Workaholic? Brokers and salesmen are workaholics.
Artists are obsessed. There's a difference."

"Your Majesty, my voyage will not only forge a new route to the spices of the East but also create over three thousand new jobs."

"*Other folks have to pay taxes, too, Mr. Herndon, so would you please spare us the dramatics!*"

"All those in favor say 'Aye.'"

"Aye."   "Aye."   "Aye."   "Aye."   "Aye."

"Actually, I preferred 'Heaven,' too, but then the marketing guys got hold of it."

"*And now at this point in the meeting I'd like to shift the blame away from me and onto someone else.*"

"This CD player costs less than players selling for twice as much."

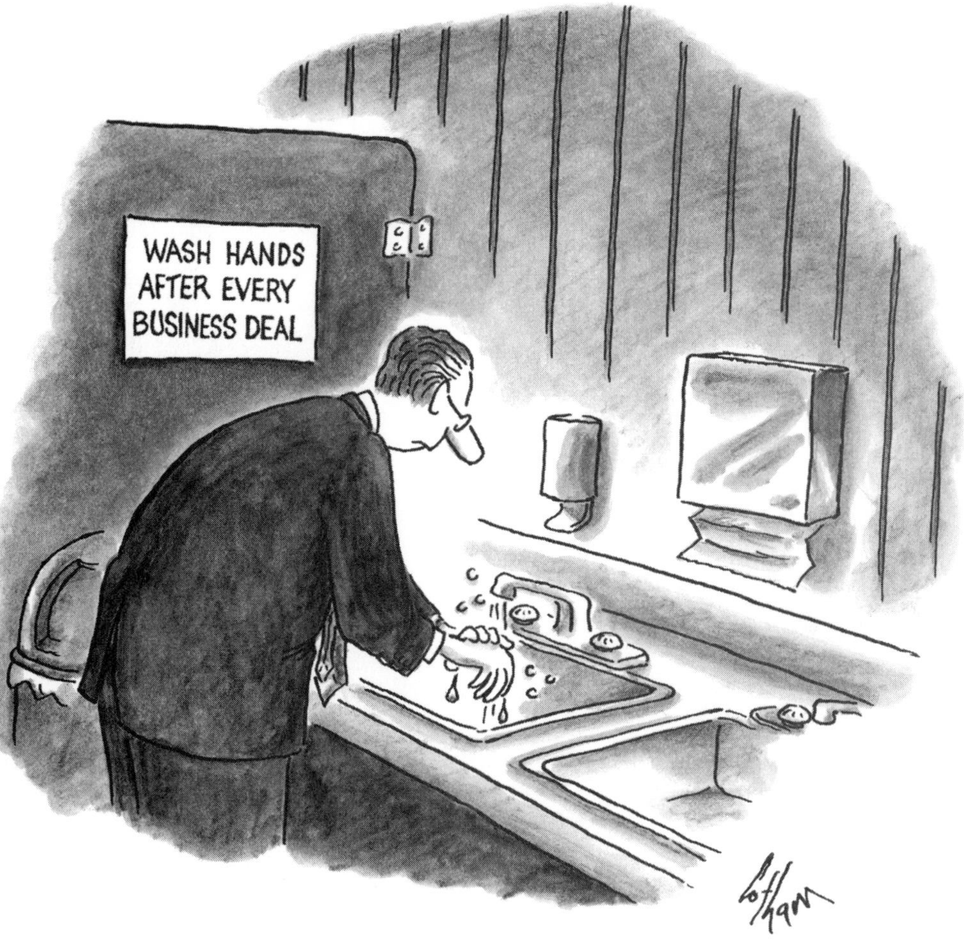
WASH HANDS
AFTER EVERY
BUSINESS DEAL

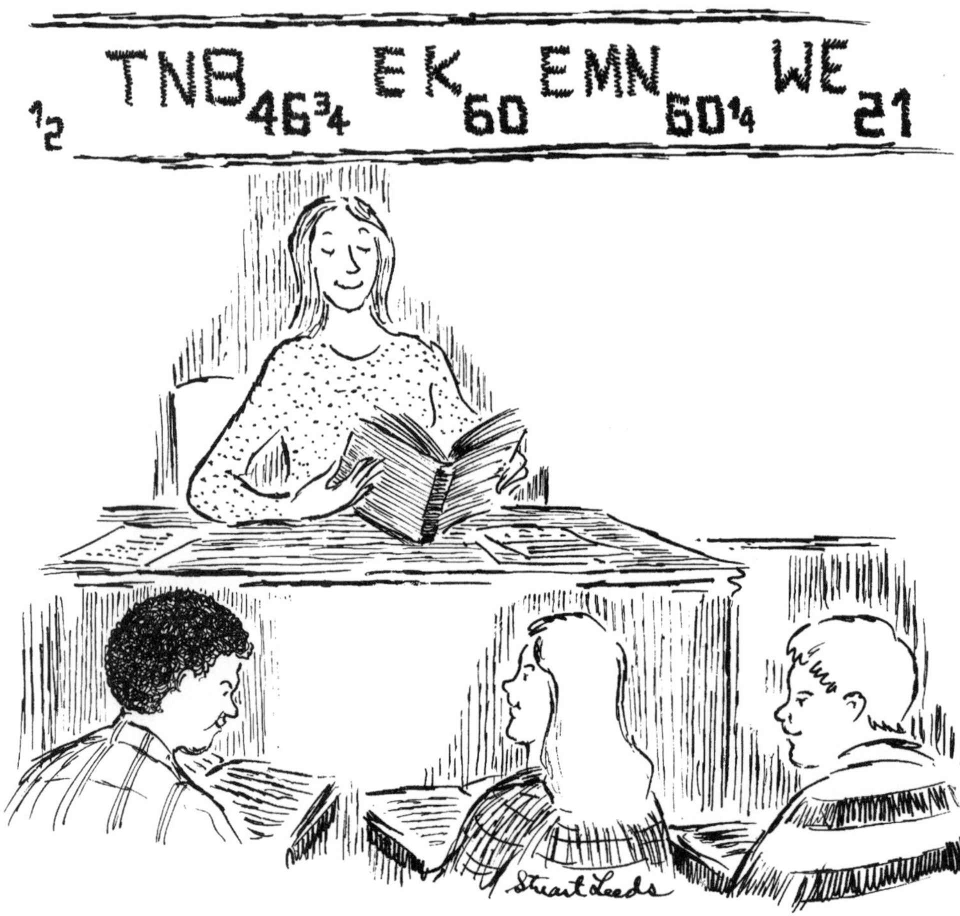
1/2 TNB 46 3/4 EK 60 EMN 60 1/4 WE 21
Stuart Leeds

CORPORATE RESPONSIBILITY
SUGGESTED GUIDELINES
① Each employee shall be allotted a desk, a chair, a telephone, a computer, and miscellaneous office supplies, as long as job lasts.
Is this all for me?
② Company shall provide janitorial services free of charge to current employees.
Last night, that wastebasket was full, and NOW IT'S EMPTY!
③ Payment of salary is the sole responsibility of employer until employee is discontinued.
So I just do my job, and then they give me money! NEAT!
④ In the event of job cessation, it is up to the company to provide that information to the terminee.
Say, guess what?

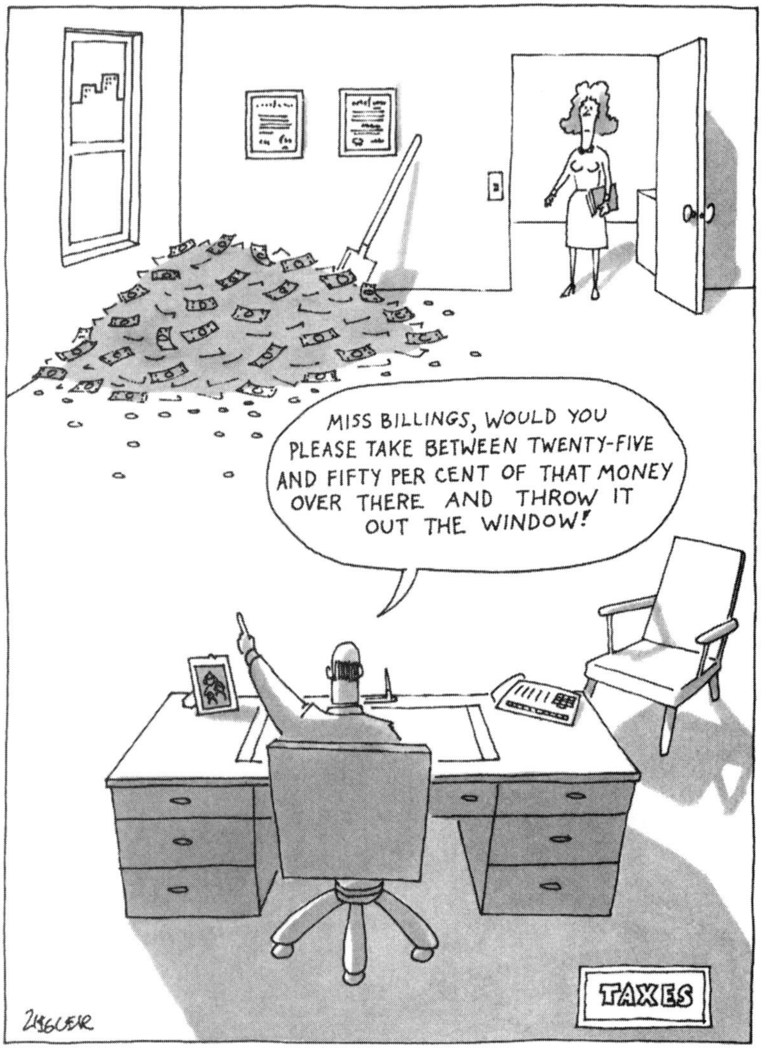
MISS BILLINGS, WOULD YOU PLEASE TAKE BETWEEN TWENTY-FIVE AND FIFTY PER CENT OF THAT MONEY OVER THERE AND THROW IT OUT THE WINDOW!
TAXES
ZIEGLER

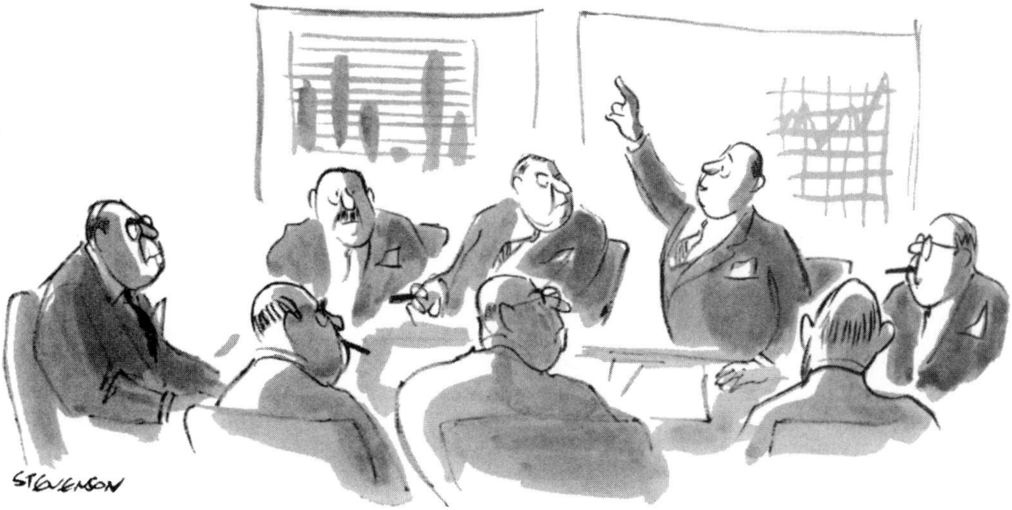

STEVENSON

"What's a debenture?"

"Before I forget, Detrick, here's the dental plan."

BEES

WORKER

QUEEN

DRONE

CONSULTANT

mcrawford

"This is the part of capitalism I hate."

"*My God, there's been a terrible accident in our Chicago office!*"

"So _that's_ where it goes! Well, I'd like to thank you fellows
for bringing this to my attention."

"You know what I think, folks? Improving technology isn't important. Increased profits aren't important. What's important is to be warm, decent human beings."

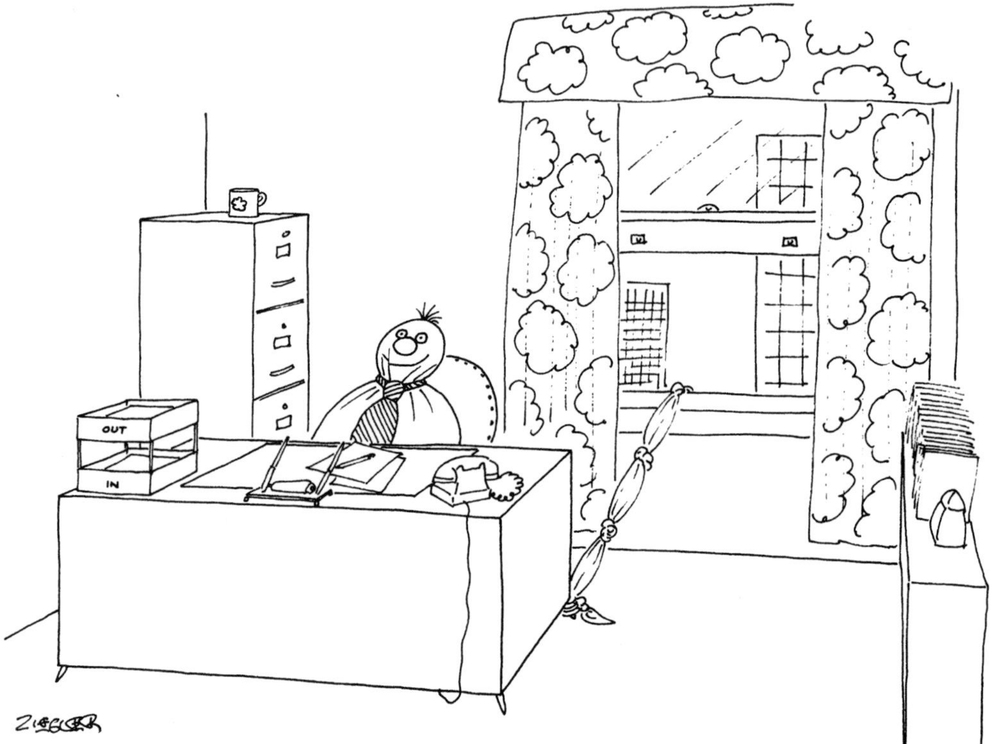
OUT
IN
ZIEGLER

"My strength is as the strength of ten, because I'm rich."

"Stop whining or this is your last Take Our Daughters to Work Day."

"*The figures for the last quarter are in. We made significant gains in the fifteen-to-twenty-six-year-old age group, but we lost our immortal souls.*"

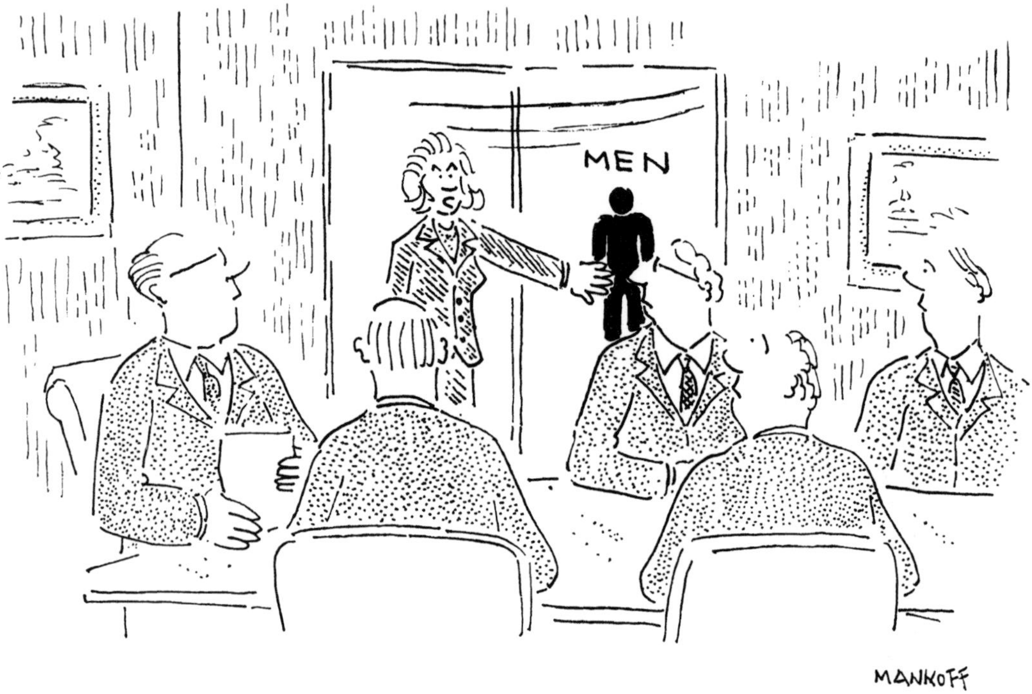
MEN
MANKOFF

"Aha! Just as I suspected!"

"You realize, of course, that any attempt on my part to profit by this information would put me at risk of an investigation by the S.E.C."

"When I agreed to the merger, Fairchild, I never contemplated this!"

"Human Resources."

"Frankly, a zillion still sounds high."

"We're just like one big happy family here."

"This year, I'm putting all my money into money."

"Now, that's the kind of innovative thinking I'd like to see around <u>our</u> shop."

"I usually wake up screaming at six-thirty, and
I'm in my office by nine."

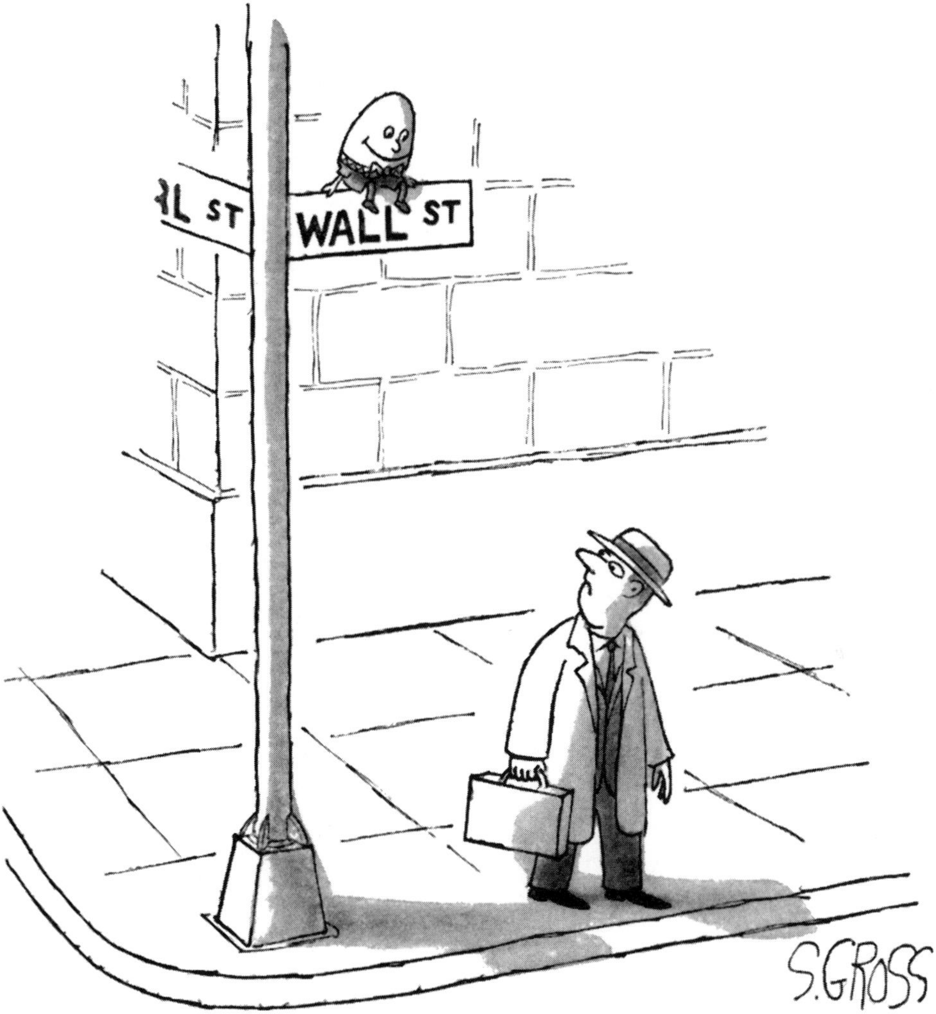
WALL ST
S.GROSS

"I can tell you one thing. Being rich beyond one's wildest
dreams doesn't go as far as it once did."

"You've been with us a long time, Winnie, and we're prepared
to offer you a generous severance package."

"Mr. Smith's office doesn't have a door.
You have to batter your way through the wall."

"*Fertig here is one of our most reliable men.*"

FORTUNE COOKIE   FORBES COOKIE   BUSINESS WEEK COOKIE

YOU WILL MEET A TALL, DARK TAX SHELTER.

BEHIND EVERY SUCCESSFUL MULTINATIONAL CORPORATION, THERE'S A TAKEOVER SPECIALIST.

WHERE THERE'S A WILL, THERE'S AN ESTATE TAX.

CRAWFORD

"I like to think of myself as a nice guy. Naturally, sometimes you have to step on a few faces."

*"And after the prime rate declined by half a point, and the Dow rose
by thirty-two, guess what happened to Goose and Fox?"*

"Money is life's report card."

"It's not you, Rob. It's just that things are moving a little too fast."

*"Then it's moved and seconded that
the compulsory retirement age be advanced to ninety-five."*

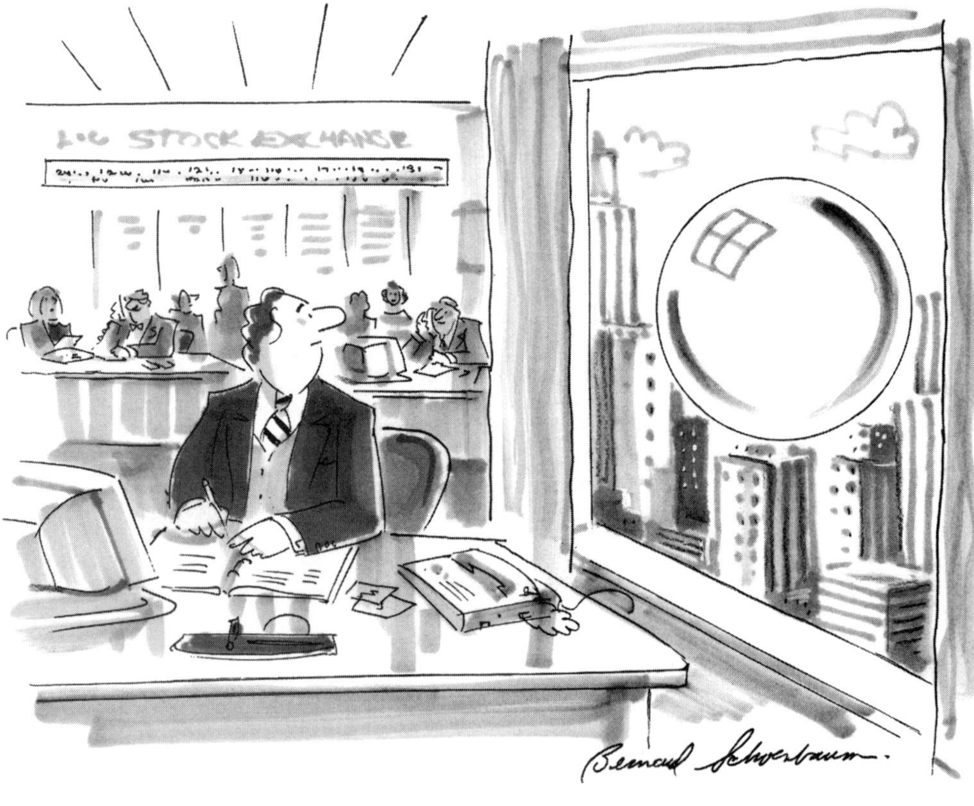
STOCK EXCHANGE

INDEX OF ARTISTS